Developing

literacy

Skills

USING STORIES

KEY STAGE 2 Y3–4 P4–5

FRANCES MACKAY

Contents

Published by Hopscotch Educational Publishing Company Ltd, 8 Severn Close, Leamington Spa CV32 7BZ.

© 1998 Hopscotch Educational Publishing

Written by Frances Mackay
Series design by Blade Communications
Illustrated by Susan Hutchison
Cover illustration by Susan Hutchison
Printed by Clintplan, Southam

Frances Mackay hereby asserts her moral right to be identified as the author of this work in accordance with the Copyright, Designs and Patents Act, 1988.

ISBN 1-902239-01-6

Introduction

◆ ABOUT THE SERIES ◆

Developing Literacy Skills is a series of books aimed at developing key literacy skills using stories, non-fiction, poetry and rhyme, spelling and grammar, from Key Stage 1 (P1–3) through to Key Stage 2 (P4–7).

The series offers a structured approach which provides detailed lesson plans to teach specific literacy skills. A unique feature of the series is the provision of differentiated photocopiable activities aimed at considerably reducing teacher preparation time. Suggestions for using the photocopiable pages as a stimulus for further work in the classroom is provided to ensure maximum use of this resource.

◆ ABOUT THIS BOOK ◆

This book is for teachers of children at Key Stage 2 Y3–4 and Scottish levels P4–5. It aims to:

◆ develop children's literacy skills through exposure to and experience of a wide range of stimulating literature with supporting differentiated activities which are both diversified and challenging;
◆ support teachers by providing practical teaching methods based on whole-class, group, paired and individual teaching;
◆ encourage enjoyment and curiosity as well as developing skills of interpretation and response.

◆ CHAPTER CONTENT ◆

Overall aims

These outline the aims for both lessons set out in each chapter.

Featured books

This lists the books used in the lessons together with story synopses or reasons for using particular texts.

Intended learning

This sets out the specific aims for each individual lesson within the chapter.

Starting point

This provides ideas for introducing the activity and may include key questions to ask the children.

Activity

This explains the task(s) the children will carry out in the lesson without supporting photocopiable activities.

Using the differentiated activity sheets

This explains how to use each sheet as well as providing guidance on the type of child who will benefit most from each sheet.

Plenary session

This suggests ideas for whole-class sessions to discuss the learning outcomes and follow-up work.

Using the photocopiable sheets as a stimulus for further work

This is a useful list of further activities that can be developed from the activity sheets. These ideas maximise the use of the photocopiable pages.

Other ideas for using ...

This contains other ideas for using the genre of books explored in each chapter. The ideas will have completely different learning intentions from the featured lessons and provide a range of alternatives.

And finally...

At the end of the book is a list of all the texts used in the chapters so that teachers have access to the publishing details.

Overall aims

✦ For children to identify a range of story settings and relate them to their own experiences.
✦ To write about similar settings.
✦ To discuss and plan main points as a structure for writing.

 Featured books

The Secret Garden
by Frances Hodgson Burnett
Danny The Champion of the World
by Roald Dahl
I'll Take You To Mrs Cole!
by Nigel Gray and Michael Foreman

Stories synopses:The Secret Garden features an historical home setting, *Danny The Champion of the World* a caravan home setting and *I'll take You to Mrs Cole* a modern home setting.

 **LESSON ONE**

 Intended learning

✦ To compare a range of story settings – writing own feelings about the extracts and discussing the words and phrases used which set the scene.

 Starting point

Read the following extracts from each book to the class. It would be a good idea to cover the book titles so that the children do not know the story titles at the beginning of the lesson. Tell them that you are going to read them an extract from three different books. Ask them to listen carefully to find out what is being described in the extracts and to decide whether they think the story is set in the past or present day.

 From *The Secret Garden*, read the end of Chapter 3 and the beginning of Chapter 4 which describes Mary's arrival at Misselthwaite Manor and her bedroom.
✦ From *Danny The Champion of the World*, read the last eight paragraphs of Chapter 1, which describe the caravan in which Danny lives.
✦ From *I'll Take You to Mrs Cole!*, read the eight pages that describe Mrs Cole's house (In the hall...)

 Key questions

Ask the children to write down which extract appealed to them most and why. Share everyone's ideas and then ask the following questions:
Q Which story was set in the past? How do you know?
Q What words/phrases used helped you to decide?
Q How did the extracts make you feel?
Q Which house would you like to live in? Why?
Q Why do you think the houses were described in detail in these stories? Does it help the reader to get a better 'feel' for the story?

 Activity

Divide the class into three groups, concentrating on one extract each. Ask them to draw a picture of what they think the house/room might look like and write five words to describe it. Encourage them to use dictionaries/word banks to collect suitable words.

 **Plenary session**

Bring the whole class together again to look at the pictures and compare them. Are the words used to describe each house similar? Show them the books the extracts were from. Are the pictures in *I'll Take You to Mrs Cole!* how they imagined them? Make a display of the children's drawings together with a copy of the extract they depict. Refer to the orginal texts – do the words accurately reflect the descriptions?

◆ LESSON TWO ◆

 Intended learning

◆ To write a description of own homes, using a planning sheet.

 Starting point

Remind the children about the three extracts read earlier. Tell them that they are now going to plan a description of their own home. Ask them to write five words to describe their home. They should use a dictionary or thesaurus to help them. Share their responses and compare them with the five words used to describe the story homes from Lesson 1. Explain that these words will help them to build up a good description of their home. (NB – This might be a sensitive issue for some children, such as those from homeless families, so they could describe a home in a well-known story instead.)

 Using the differentiated activity sheets

Provide the children with the appropriate activity sheet and ask them to write their five words in the space provided. Explain that these planning sheets will help them to write their final description.

Activity sheet 1

This is aimed at those children who need support with vocabulary and find writing more difficult.

Activity sheet 2

This is aimed at those children who can write more independently.

Activity sheet 3

This is aimed at those children who are more able writers.

◆ As the children complete the task, they could draw a picture of their home to add to the display of drawings already completed after Lesson 1.

◆ When they have completed the sheets, bring the whole class together again. Share their answers. Explain that they will use these planning sheets to write a more detailed description of their home as if describing it to someone who has never been there. (This may need to be carried out in a third lesson if this seems more appropriate.)

◆ Discuss what they want the reader to know about their home – how it feels, what it looks like, what goes on there and so on.

◆ Reread some of the extracts if you think it necessary to remind the children how writers can use words to convey meaning and feelings. Ask the children to try and build on these ideas and use them in their writing.

 Plenary session

Ask the children to read out their writing to others. Ask them to suggest good points about each one – words and phrases that they liked and why. The words could be categorised under specific headings to build up word banks. Words of similar meanings could be explored – which of them is the more appropriate? Discuss how their writing could be improved. Add the writing to the display of pictures of homes.

Stories with everyday settings

USING THE PHOTOCOPIABLE SHEETS AS A STIMULUS FOR FURTHER WORK

◆ Write Estate Agents' advertisements for the homes. Discuss point of view – what is fact and what is opinion in advertisements?

◆ Make up lists of adjectives to describe the rooms in homes, using the planning sheets as a starting point. Display the words in a house-shaped poster.

roomy   spacious
nice   outlook
charming   fitted

◆ Make up a list of home improvements using the facts stated as a guide. Use magazines to cut out pictures to show what the new rooms would look like!

◆ Draw pictures of particular rooms described. Write adjectives from the activity sheet to display around the picture.

◆ Compare a room from a story (for example, Mary's bedroom in *The Secret Garden*) with the children's own descriptions.

◆ Play 'Where am I?'. Ask the children to read out descriptions for others to guess which room it is.

OTHER IDEAS FOR USING STORIES WITH EVERYDAY SETTINGS

◆ Compare stories about school life with 'real' school situations. How accurate/inaccurate are they?

◆ Read stories about families. Make up a class 'photo' album of drawings that depict things that have happened to the family in the story. Write sentences about each 'photo'. Ask the children to bring along their own photos and write their own sentences to compare real and imaginary families.

◆ Use stories to stimulate anecdotal writing from the children, such as what happened to them in similar incidents/experiences.

◆ Rewrite the stories by asking the children to write themselves as one of the characters – How would I have responded? How would the story change?

◆ Write new events in the same settings or change the beginning or ending.

◆ Make a collection of words or phrases from the books that the children read which describe an everyday setting, such as school or home life.

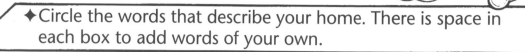

My home

✦Circle the words that describe your home. There is space in each box to add words of your own.

My home is:

medium   new   caravan
cement   small   stone
wooden   boat

My bedroom is:

big   medium   untidy   cold   sunny
bright   dark   dull   papered

It has:

bed   cupboards   wooden floor
television   computer

My living room is:

sunny   big   medium   colourful
dull   untidy   horrible

It has:

video   settee   table   books
carpet   a good view

Use a dictionary to help you to find five words that describe your home.

_____

_____

_____

_____

My kitchen is:

old   new   warm   big

It has:

fridge   table   sink   stools
washing machine   tiles

My home

◆ Write about your home in the spaces provided.

My home is:

_____
_____
_____
_____
_____
_____

My bedroom is:

_____
_____
_____
_____
_____
_____
_____
_____

My living room is:

_____
_____
_____
_____
_____
_____

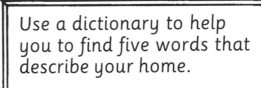

Use a dictionary to help you to find five words that describe your home.

_____
_____
_____
_____
_____

My kitchen is:

_____
_____
_____
_____
_____

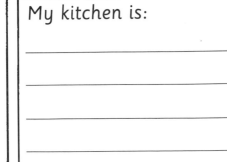

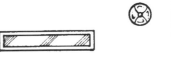

Developing
literacy
Skills

✦ My home ✦

✦Describe what your home looks like on the outside.

_____

_____

✦Describe the rooms inside your home.

_____

_____

_____

_____

_____

_____

✦What is good about your home?

_____

_____

✦What is bad about your home?

_____

_____

✦How do you feel in your home?

_____

_____

Use a dictionary and thesaurus to help you to find five words that describe your home.

_____

_____

_____

_____

Dialogue

 ## Overall aims

- ✦ To categorise different types of dialogue, such as questions, commands and statements.
- ✦ To dramatise stories by acting them out.
- ✦ To write some dialogue.

 ## Activities

- ✦ Act out Chapter 3 with the teacher as narrator and the children acting out the speaking parts. It is not necessary to use exact dialogue from the text – the children could make up their own to match the storyline. Discuss how voices change for different types of dialogue, such as questions, surprise and commands. Encourage the children to use these intonations in their dialogue responses.
- ✦ Then divide the class into groups and ask them to write what they think the next chapter in the story will be about. Tell them to keep the chapter short and use all three kinds of dialogue in their writing. Make sure each group contains a child capable of being a group scribe. This activity could be differentiated to prepare the children for Lesson 2. For example, one group could draw the chapter using speech bubbles, one group could write a playscript and the third group could write story dialogue.

 ## Featured book

Chocolate Fever
by Robert Kimmel Smith

Story synopsis: Henry is always eating chocolate and one day he becomes covered in large, brown, chocolate spots. He is inspected by all the doctors at the local hospital and is teased by a gang of boys so he decides to run away. He is picked up by a truck driver and then kidnapped by thieves, but he eventually finds a cure for the spots.

 ## Intended learning

- ✦ To identify and classify dialogue into different types.
- ✦ To dramatise a story.

 ## Starting point

Read Chapters 2 and 3 of *Chocolate Fever* to the class. Ask the children to predict what they think might happen in the story. Tell them you will complete the story at another time but today you will be looking at the dialogue in the story. Discuss the different types of dialogue – question, command and statement – and ask the children to make up examples of each kind. Talk about the types of punctuation used to show each type. Copy out an enlarged version of some of the text and use this to identify for the children examples of the type of dialogue and the punctuation.

 ## Plenary session

Bring the whole class together again to watch each group act out their chapter. Stop the group occasionally to ask the audience what type of dialogue is being used. Discuss the story ideas and outcomes – how similar or different are they? Read the next chapter in *Chocolate Fever* to find out what really happens.

Dialogue

◆ LESSON TWO ◆

◆ Intended learning

◆ To write some dialogue using text or illustrations as a starting point.

◆ Starting points

Remind the children about the discussion on types of dialogue covered in Lesson 1. Write up several examples on the board for them to classify to ensure they remember and understand.

Ask the children to tell you of examples where dialogue might be found – story books, plays, comic strips, newspaper articles, magazine interviews, poetry and so on. Provide the children with appropriate texts containing such examples. Allow them time to explore the texts in pairs then discuss how the use of dialogue differs in each, for example the use of shorter sentences and lots of exclamations in comics and how the settings of playscript dialogue differs from story book dialogue, and so on.

◆ Using the differentiated activity sheets

Explain to the children that they are now going to try writing dialogue for different purposes. One group will be writing a comic strip, one group a play and the third group a story.

Activity sheet 1

This is aimed at those children who need picture clues to help them write a story.

Activity sheet 2

This is aimed at those children who can write more independently and can use text as a starting point.

Activity sheet 3

This is aimed at more able writers who are able to use a variety of dialogue types and can recognise the use of dialect and characterisation.

◆ Plenary session

After the children have completed the activity sheets bring the whole class together again. Explain the different tasks that each group had to do and ask one or two children from each group to read out or say what happened in their stories. Talk about how one story outline can have a large variety of different outcomes.

Discuss the different forms of presenting dialogue – speech bubbles, play scripts and speech marks. Do the presentational formats they have used match the text examples looked at earlier? Which format do they prefer to write/read? Why? What difficulties did they encounter? Talk about how these problems might be overcome.

Dialogue

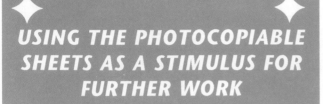

USING THE PHOTOCOPIABLE SHEETS AS A STIMULUS FOR FURTHER WORK

✦ Ask each group to rewrite their story in a different format, for example ask the comic strip group to rewrite theirs as a play. Discuss the different approach needed for presenting the story this way.

✦ Make the comic strips into a class book, add other comic strips of the children's own invention.

✦ Act out the plays produced by group 2. Encourage the children to write their own short play about a holiday adventure.

✦ Look at story books to see how dialogue is presented. Compare them with the stories written by group 3 – how could their presentation be improved?

✦ Cut up the comic strip into squares. Ask the children to write a picture book with added writing to link the comic strip pictures together as a story.

✦ Have fun reading out the holiday play in different accents or voices!

OTHER IDEAS FOR USING DIALOGUE

✦ Dramatise the story using puppets or costumes and masks.

✦ Make a television programme using pictures and 'off-screen' voice-overs.

✦ Use playscripts for shared reading to practise intonation and characterisation.

✦ Compare how settings are written into playscripts – what devices are used, how is the reader informed of the setting?

✦ Use picture books with no text to encourage the children to write their own – use paper and a temporary adhesive to fix speech bubbles to the pages.

✦ Cut up a copy of a short play into sections – can the children put it together in the right sequence so that it makes sense? Is there more than one possibility?

✦ Encourage the use of playscripts as reading books – take it in turns to 'act out' the text when listening to the child read.

✦ Rewrite favourite stories as plays – let one group prepare and act them out to the rest of the class – can others guess the book?

✦ Read out the dialogue of characters from books – can the children guess the character?

✦ Compare versions of the same story. Does the dialogue vary? Why has it changed?

The holiday

✦ Fill in the words that you think the characters in this cartoon strip are saying.

✦ On the back of this sheet, draw and write another episode to this story.

◆ The holiday ◆

◆ This is a play about a family holiday. Write in the words that you think the characters might say.

Narrator:	Mr and Mrs Brown and their nine-year-old daughter, Jane, have just arrived at their hotel in Cornwall for a two-week holiday. Jane has never been to Cornwall before and is looking forward to spending time on the beach.
Mr Brown:	Come on, Jane, hurry up. We need to get everything unpacked.
Jane:	_____
Mrs Brown:	Oh, look at the lovely view! I can't wait to get onto the beach!
Jane:	Can't we leave the unpacking, Dad, and walk along the beach?
Mr Brown:	_____
Mrs Brown:	Look at the water. It looks very inviting. I think I'll have a paddle.
Narrator:	Mr and Mrs Brown walk to the water's edge but Jane runs on ahead. Soon she is nowhere to be seen.
Mr and Mrs Brown:	Jane! Jane! Where are you?
Mr Brown:	_____
Mrs Brown:	_____
Narrator:	Suddenly they see Jane. She has climbed to the top of a cliff and is waving to them.
Mrs Brown:	Jane! Be careful!

◆ Now, complete the play on the back of this sheet.

Photocopiable

◆ The holiday ◆

◆ This is the beginning of a story. Read it and then finish it. Remember to use speech marks, question marks, exclamation marks and full stops.

"C'mon, will ya! We're gunna be late!" Robbie shouted at this brother.

"OK, OK! Keep your hair on!" answered Tom.

Robbie and Tom's mother smiled to herself because the boys were always arguing but she knew that Robbie really cared for his younger brother but didn't want to show it.

"Come on, you two. Onto the train now," she said.

They travelled for hours up on to the Yorkshire Moors, finally reaching Garsdale Head station late in the afternoon.

"Look, they've sent Lilian to meet us," said Mum. "Hello there, we've finally made it!"

"Aye – and what does tha think of moors, then?" asked Lilian of the two boys.

"It's very bare," said Robbie.

"Ah, well. Tha'll soon get used to it," laughed Lilian. "I'm sure tha'll be runnin' all over moors soon enough."

Little did the boys realise just how much they would come to know the moors in the coming week. If they knew then that they would spend three days alone, lost on the moors, they would never have agreed to come in the first place.

This is how it happened …

◆ Continue on the back of this sheet.

Overall aims

◆ To identify and discuss the main and recurring characters in traditional tales.
◆ To evaluate the behaviour of characters and to write a character portrait.

 Featured book

The King's Equal
by Katherine Paterson

Story synopsis: The old King is dying and, because he realises that his son, Raphael, is greedy and selfish, he decrees that after his death Raphael can only become King if he marries a woman who equals him in appearance, intelligence and wealth. Raphael sends out many messengers to find such a woman but their attempts fail. A magic wolf brings Rosamund, a farmer's daughter, to the castle. Raphael is spellbound by her and wants to marry her. Rosamund sets Raphael a challenge and, helped by the wolf, his character changes for the better and they finally wed.

 Intended learning

◆ To identify and discuss the main characters in traditional tales.
◆ To evaluate the behaviour of characters and write a character portrait as a class.

 Questions to ask

Read the story *The King's Equal* to the class. Ask the children the following questions to find out what they already know about traditional tales.

Q Does the story remind you of other stories you have heard or read? In what ways is it similar?

Q What kinds of characters are usually found in traditional tales? Does this book have some of these characters?
Q What are Kings/princes/princesses usually like?
Q Who are usually the 'baddies'/'goodies'?
Q What usually happens to the baddies?

Record the children's contributions for a class display. This could be added to a data bank on traditional tales.

 Group activities

Divide the children into small groups to discuss the following questions. Appoint a group scribe to make notes about the group's decisions.
◆ Who are the good and bad characters in *The King's Equal*?
◆ Do you think the king made a wise decision to make his son marry a particular kind of woman? Explain why/why not.
◆ How would you describe Raphael's character before he met Rosamund? How did he treat people? Why do you think he behaved like this? Would you have liked to have met him?
◆ Why do you think Rosamund was kind and caring even though she was very poor?
◆ Why do you think Raphael's character changed after spending time with the wolf? What kinds of things did the wolf teach him?

 Plenary session

Bring the whole class together again. Share the groups' ideas. Write a character portrait of Raphael together, with the teacher acting as scribe. Use the illustrations in the book as a guide to describe what he looks like and the clothes he wore. Use passages from the book to illustrate his behaviour.

Read out the finished description. Does everyone agree that it describes Raphael well? Has anything important been left out? Could better words/phrases be used to improve the writing?

◆LESSON TWO◆

◆ Intended learning

◆ To compare the role of the wolf in different traditional tales.
◆ To write a character portrait of the wolf in pairs or individually using the photocopiable pages.

◆ Starting point

Summarise what the children have discovered about the characters in traditional tales so far. Remind them how they helped to write a character portrait of Raphael. Tell them that they are now going to write a character portrait of their own about a wolf.

◆ Questions to ask

Q Name some Traditional Tales with wolves in them. (Show them some relevant books to prompt their memories.) What are the wolves usually like? What do they look like? How do they usually behave?

Q What things do the wolves often do in these stories? What usually happens to them in the end?

◆ Using the differentiated activity sheets

Explain to the children that they will now work in pairs or individually to consider the wolf's character in more detail.

Activity sheet 1

This is aimed at those children who need support with vocabulary and sentence structure.

Activity sheet 2

This is aimed at those children who can write independently but may need some teacher support.

Activity sheet 3

This is aimed at those children who are more able writers and have experience of reading/listening to tales with wolves in them.

◆ Plenary session

Bring the whole class together to discuss their work. Ask some children to read out their descriptions of the wolf. Are they similar in any way? Discuss the words used to describe the wolf's looks and behaviour. Ask the following questions:

◆ Why do you think authors write wolves as bad characters in their stories?

◆ What about in *The King's Equal*? How different is this wolf? Do you know of any other stories where the wolf is a good one? Does *The King's Equal* change the way we might think about wolves? (Encourage the children to develop an awareness of the need to challenge stereotypes by referring them to alternative stories such as *Cinderella and the Hot Air Balloon* by Ann Jungman and *Princess Smartypants* and *Prince Cinders* by Babette Cole.)

◆ Why do you think authors of traditional tales write stories about good and bad characters? Are the books supposed to teach us something? What do you think the message might be in *The King's Equal*?

Traditional tales

USING THE PHOTOCOPIABLE SHEETS AS A STIMULUS FOR FURTHER WORK

✦ Ask the children to draw a wolf from a traditional tale and use their writing from the photocopiable activity to help them write a paragraph about the wolf they have drawn. The work could be displayed together with the storybooks.

✦ Make a 'rogues gallery' of wanted posters of bad characters from traditional tales, including the wolf. Write a description of each one plus a list of the 'crimes' committed and who wants to capture them.

✦ Hot seating – ask the children to become a wolf from a traditional tale. Ask him/her questions. The child must stay in role and answer as if they were the character.

✦ Write a letter from one wolf to another, such as from the wolf in Little Red Riding Hood to the wolf in *The King's Equal*. What might they say to each other? If the letters are left unsigned, others could try and work out which stories the wolves are from.

OTHER IDEAS FOR USING TRADITIONAL TALES

✦ Play 'Who am I?'. One child describes a character from a tale and the others have to guess who it is.

✦ Using a collection of traditional tales, ask the children to work in pairs or small groups to look at the beginnings and endings. Are they similar in any way? Why is this so? Are particular words or phrases often used? Are the endings always happy ones? Why do they think this is so?

✦ Make 'Good as Gold' awards for the 'goodies' in traditional tales. Ask the children to draw a picture of the character and write why they have received this award.

✦ Role play – ask the children to act out a character. Can the others guess who it is?

✦ Provide the children with the beginning of a tale. Can they complete it, orally or in writing?

✦ Ask the children to write a traditional beginning or ending for a story. How do they compare?

✦ Ask the children to discuss why certain characters behave as they do in the stories. Can their behaviour be justified in some way? What would the children do if they were the character? How would they respond?

✦ Read alternative tales. How do they compare with the originals? Discuss why alternative tales may have been written – to amuse, to address gender issues, and so on.

✦ The wolf ... ✦

✦ Circle the words that describe this wolf. Add some words of your own.

pretty   ugly

friendly   big ears

mean   brave

hairy   tongue

frightening   sharp

✦ Finish the drawing of this wolf.

✦ Circle the words that describe what the wolf might do. Add some ideas of your own.

pick flowers   sing songs

scare somebody

eat someone   do a dance

snarl   bite

✦ Use words from the lists as well as your own words to finish these sentences.

The wolf is called _____

He lives _____

His face is _____

His teeth are _____

His body is _____

He looks _____

He likes to _____

The wolf is going to _____

_____

Then he will _____

_____

The wolf ...

✦ Look at this picture of a wolf. Write some sentences to describe what he looks like. Use a dictionary and thesaurus to help you.

_____

_____

_____

_____

✦ Write what you think the rest of the wolf's body looks like.

_____

_____

✦ What kind of character is this wolf? Is he kind or cruel? Write some sentences to describe how he behaves.

_____

_____

_____

✦ What kinds of things does the wolf like to do? _____

_____

✦ Who is he going to meet one day? _____

✦ What do you think will happen? _____

_____

_____

20 **Using Stories**
KS2: Y3–4/P4–5

Developing
literacy
skills

Photocopiable

◆ The wolf ... ◆

◆ Write down the name of a traditional tale that has a wolf in it.

_____

◆ Describe what the wolf was like in the story.

_____
_____
_____

◆ Why do you think the author put a wolf in the story?

_____
_____
_____

◆ What did the wolf do in this story?

_____
_____
_____

◆ What happened to the wolf in the end?

_____

◆ Do you think this was a good ending to the story? Why/why not?

_____
_____

◆ If you were writing a story with a wolf in it,
would the wolf be good or bad?   _____

◆ On the back of this sheet, describe what your wolf would look like and how
he or she would behave. Use a dictionary and thesaurus to help you.

Myths, legends and fables

 Overall aims

- To identify common themes, such as trials and forfeits.
- For the children to write a story plan for their own myth, using different characters or settings.

 Featured book

The Orchard Book of Greek Myths
retold by Geraldine McCaughrean

Book synopsis: This is a collection of sixteen Greek myths, telling the stories of Pandora's Box, Persephone, Narcissus, Daedalus and Icarus, Arachne, King Midas, Perseus, Heracles, Apollo, Theseus, Jason, Orpheus, Atalanta, Wooden Horse of Troy, Odysseus and Prometheus.

 **LESSON ONE**

 Intended learning

- To identify and discuss common themes in the stories.
- To discuss the reasons behind these stories being told.

 Starting point

Read the class some of the stories from the book. Ask them the following questions to find out what they already know about myths, legends and fables.
- What is a myth or legend?
- Can you name other myths and legends not in this book? Where did you hear them?
- Why do you think these stories have been told? Do they have a special purpose?
- What is a fable? Do you know any? Do they have a special message? Why do you think they were written?
- What might be the differences between myths and legends and fables?

 Do you think the stories from *The Orchard Book* have any special messages for the reader? Do they have any particular theme? In which ones do the wise win over the foolish, for example?

 Activities

Divide the children into pairs or small groups to discuss and record the following:
- Choose one of the stories. Decide as a group what the main theme is – either wise over foolish, trials and forfeits, good over evil, strong over weak or another theme.
- Write down who the main characters are. Draw a circle around the names and add labels to show their character, strengths, weaknesses, role in the story (show an example).
- Decide what it was that set the action in motion – what it because someone was jealous of another? Was it due to greed/love/hatred?
- Make a list/map of the key events in the order in which they happened in the story.

Plenary session

Bring the whole class together again to share what they found out.
- Why did they choose the story? Did they enjoy this one best? Why?
- What themes did they find? Was it easy to agree as a group?
- Are the two main characters usually total opposites in character and personality? Do you think this helps the story in some way? How?
- Was it difficult to remember the sequence of events? Did you need to refer back to the story? Did you miss out anything important?
- Did you learn anything about people's behaviour from this story? Do you think that is why the story was written/told? How would you have reacted in the same situation?

LESSON TWO

 Intended learning

◆ To plan own myth, using a traditional theme but substituting the characters and settings into a modern-day setting.

 Starting point

Summarise what the children have discovered so far about the themes and characters in myths and legends. Tell them that they are now going to work with one of the stories in particular, 'The Twelve Labours of Heracles'.

Questions to ask

Q What do you think of this story?
Q What is the main theme? Who was wise/foolish?
Q What were all the trials Heracles had to perform? List them.
Q How did he solve some of them? What do you think of his solutions?
Q Would you have thought of different/better ones?
Q What kinds of trials might Heracles be given in today's world?

Using the differentiated activity sheets

Explain to the children that they will now have the opportunity to write their own version of 'The Trials of Heracles' in pairs or individually. Tell them that instead of using a Greek setting in the past, they will be using a modern-day setting, changing the characters and trials to suit themselves! Tell them that the photocopiable sheet will be used as a story planner to help them in this task. It may be necessary to explain the sheets to each group before they commence work and you may wish to group together those children using Activity sheet 1 in order to give more support.

Activity sheet 1

This is aimed at those children who are less able writers and who need support with vocabulary and planning.

Activity sheet 2

This is aimed at those children who can write independently but need help in structuring their story plan.

Activity sheet 3

This is aimed at those children who are more able writers and need little teacher support.

 Plenary session

After each group has completed the activity, bring the whole class together to discuss their work. Ask some children to read out some of their twelve labours. What do the others think of these tasks and how they were solved? Which ones might be possible? Which ones are just pure fantasy? Compare the story endings – did the good character always win in the end? Was there a message in their story?

Discuss the use of the story planning sheet – how did it help them? How will they use it to write their story?

Finally, ask the children to write their stories individually or in pairs. Make them into books for everyone to share.

Make a collection of books on Myths, legends and fables and encourage the children to add to it.

Myths, legends and fables

◆ USING THE PHOTOCOPIABLE SHEETS AS A STIMULUS FOR FURTHER WORK ◆

✦ Use the sheets to improve story lines. Ask the children to work in pairs to read out some of the twelve labours to each other. How would their partner solve the task? Is this a better solution than the one first thought of? Can the partner help to suggest better ideas for a task?

✦ Use the planning pages to discuss story beginnings and endings in more detail as a whole class. What makes a good/exciting beginning? What sort of endings can stories have – happy? sad? unexpected? funny?

✦ Use the ideas to write a whole class or group story to model the story writing process.

✦ Ask the children to paint/draw some of the labours to create a display to go with the stories.

✦ Use the pages as a prompt sheet to tell the story on to a tape.

✦ Use the sheets to write a playscript of the story.

◆ OTHER IDEAS FOR USING MYTHS, LEGENDS AND FABLES ◆

✦ Read the beginnings of different stories – how do they compare? Is there a similar pattern? Are particular words/phrases common? How do the beginnings of these stories compare with modern day stories?

✦ Use the common themes, such as good over evil, to discuss moral issues. Should stories try to help children decide right from wrong? Do we learn how we should behave from sharing stories? Is this a good thing? Can you justify your answer?

✦ Make storyboards, cartoon strips of the stories.

✦ Write character portraits of people from different stories – such as kind and/or selfish characters – draw them and write about their behaviour and personality. Are the drawings influenced by the character's personalities? Are bad people often depicted as ugly?

✦ Change the endings to familiar stories.

✦ Write a modern version of a fable – what things do today's children need to be aware of? (For example, stranger danger).

✦ Compare stories from different cultures – are there recurrent themes? Find out information about the country the story is from.

✦ Ask people from different cultures to tell stories to the class.

✦ Ask the children to draw a picture from a familiar story – can the others guess the story?

✦ Write a newspaper version of the tale.

✦ My story planner ✦

✦ Write your own story about the trials of Heracles. Fill in the gaps to tell the beginning of your story.

One day a baby was born in a town called _____.
The baby was called _____. The baby grew up to be
very _____ and _____. When he/she
was 20 years old a terrible thing happened. He/she was blamed
for a huge computer fault. It caused all the computers in town
to shut down. The mayor was very angry, so he ordered
_____ to carry out 12 tasks before the year was up!

✦ Now write down your 12 tasks and draw a picture of one of them.

_____

_____

_____

_____

_____

_____

_____

_____

_____

✦ On the back of this sheet draw and write how your story ends.
Use a dictionary or thesaurus to help you.

◆ My story planner ◆

Title – THE TWELVE LABOURS OF _____

◆Draw pictures of your two characters and then draw lines from each character to the words in the box that best describe them. Use a dictionary or thesaurus to find other words to add to the box.

wise

foolish   weak

young

coward   strong

happy   good   rich

ugly

Main character   **Second character**

◆Fill in the gaps below to tell the beginning of your story.

There was once a baby born in _____ (country) in a town called _____. The baby was very special because he/she was very _____. When the baby grew up, a terrible thing happened. He/she

_____

_____. For doing

this terrible thing, _____ (main character's name) was punished by _____ (second character's name). He/she had to perform 12 difficult tasks in order to be set free again.

◆On the back of this sheet, write out your 12 labours and how they were solved.

Photocopiable

◆ My story planner ◆

◆ Write the names of the characters in your story and some sentences about them. You could write about what they look like, how they behave, whether they are strong or weak, good or bad, rich or poor, wise or foolish and so on. Use a dictionary or thesaurus to help you to select the most appropriate words.

CHARACTER 1 _____

_____

_____

CHARACTER 2 _____

_____

_____

CHARACTER 3 _____

_____

_____

◆ Write about where your story is set – the time and place. Think of an exciting way to introduce the main character. What happens to make him/her have to do the 12 labours?

_____

_____

_____

_____

_____

◆ Plan what the 12 labours could be and how they could be solved. Make the tasks difficult, funny or strange. Continue on the back of this sheet.

_____

_____

_____

_____

_____

_____

Using Stories
KS2: Y3–4/P4–5

Developing
Literacy
Skills

Photocopiable

27

Adventure stories

 ## Overall aims

✦ To compare fact and fiction and the credibility of events.
✦ To discuss characters' feelings and reactions and compare them with the children's own reactions.
✦ To write a first person account of a story/incident.

 ## Featured book

The Stowaways
by Roger McGough

Story synopsis: The book centres on the everyday lives of two young boys living in Liverpool. Their adventures include running away from home and finding buried 'treasure' on a beach. The story includes four different tales in a very humorous style with simple line illustrations.

 ## ✦ LESSON ONE ✦

 ## Intended learning

✦ To identify what could be fact and what might be fiction in the story.
✦ To explore characters' feelings and reactions and compare them with the children's own reactions.

Starting points

✦ Find Liverpool on a map. Explain that the story is set in a real place but that not everything else in the story is necessarily true.
✦ Discuss 'fact' and 'fiction'. Ask the children if they think the following examples from the book are fact or fiction:

1 'In the old days (but not so long ago) the River Mersey was far busier than it is today.'
2 'Six foot six, muscles rippling in the wind, huge hands grappling with the helm, rum soaked and fierce as a wounded shark (and that was only my grandmother!).'

3 'I was the perfect child: clean, well–mannered, obedient...soft in the head.'
4 'I read somewhere that sailors lived off rum and dry biscuits.'
5 'She was older than Midge by about a hundred years.'

✦ How credible do the children think the events in the story are? Explain that they are now going to consider some of the events in more detail to compare what happened in the story with what they might do if the events happened to them.

 ## Using the differentiated activity sheets

Activity sheet 1

This is aimed at those children who need support with reading and writing and would benefit from being allowed to draw part of their answers.

Activity sheet 2

This is aimed at more independent writers who are able to respond to questions in a written form.

Activity sheet 3

This is aimed at more able children who are able to make more detailed judgements about the contents of the story.

 ## Plenary session

Bring the class together to discuss their findings. Ask some children to read or tell their responses to some of the questions.
✦ What decisions did the boys make that were good?
✦ What decisions were foolish?
✦ Why do you think they behaved as they did?

Discuss safety issues and the reasons behind making a good decision.

 LESSON TWO

◆ Intended learning

◆ To write a first person account of an incident in the book.

◆ Starting point

Ask the children to remind you what happened in the last chapter of *The Stowaways* where the boys find a metal box at the beach. Reread all or part of the chapter if necessary to refresh their memories of what happened. Ask them to tell you who they think the person 'I' is in the story. Is it the author writing about himself when he was young perhaps? Explain that some stories are written like this, where the author is part of the story, and sometimes this can make the story seem more real or true-to-life – that it actually happened.

◆ Activities

◆ Ask the children to sit in a circle and then bring out a very old, rusty metal box. Explain that this could be the very box that the two children found on the beach. Ask them to say one word each about the box to describe it.

◆ Ask the children to imagine that they had found the box on the beach, then ask the following questions. Encourage the children to invent interesting answers.

Q Where did the box come from?

Q Who owned it once?

Q How did it get on to the beach?

Q What was inside it?

Q Where should the box be now?

◆ Share the ideas to see which ones they like best. Then ask them to write the story of the box as if they had found it themselves. They could either retell the story of *The Stowaways* but change the ending or they could write a completely new chapter using any of the ideas mentioned, saying how they felt when they found the box, what they did and what happened next.

 Plenary session

Read out some of the children's work at the end of the lesson. Share good examples of writing about people's feelings and responses. Compare the different ideas for what was contained in the box and what happened to the characters. Discuss whether the stories could be credible or not – what could be fact and what would be fiction? Make the stories into books in the shape of treasure chests or put them inside a box made to look like a treasure chest. Build up a class collection of adventure stories on a similar theme.

Adventure stories

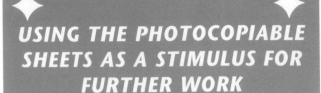

USING THE PHOTOCOPIABLE SHEETS AS A STIMULUS FOR FURTHER WORK

✦ Make other picture sequences as in Activity sheet 1 to share ideas about decision-making events, such as bullying at school or strangers approaching children at playgrounds.

✦ Make a class book entitled: 'What would you do?' with pictures and sentences about problems on one page and solutions on the other.

✦ Ask the children to draw or write about a problem they had to face and say what they did to solve it.

✦ Write about childhood memories – silly things that we did when we were very young! Start them off by telling them something that happened to you. Make them into a book with baby photographs.

✦ Write and compare lists – good and bad decisions I have made.

✦ Make a book called: 'How I feel when...' with pictures and writing about things such as getting lost, when a new baby arrives, when mum is ill and when the holidays arrive.

✦ Make a book for new children coming to the school – what to do if... – with the children writing how to solve problems sensibly and safely.

✦ Change Chapter 1 – write a story where the boys actually travel on a ship to a strange foreign land.

OTHER IDEAS FOR USING ADVENTURE STORIES

✦ Explore picture books that use illustrations to develop adventures, such as *Where the Wild Things Are* by Maurice Sendak.

✦ Draw maps of story plots – where the characters started off, where they travelled to and what they saw on the way.

✦ Discuss the relationships in the stories – what tells you they were friends/enemies? How did they help/hinder each other? Did they respond to events in the way you thought they would?

✦ Draw scenes from the book – can others guess the story?

✦ Write the adventure in a diary format, summarising days and events.

◆ The stowaways ◆

The two boys in the story have many adventures. Two of them are shown below.
◆ Draw pictures and write about what happened next. Then write and draw about what you would do if it happened to you.

The event	What they did	What you would do

The two boys get

into trouble at

school and at home.

So they decide to

_____

_____

I would

_____

_____

The event	What they did	What you would do

The boys find a black,

rusty metal box at the

beach.

So they decide to

_____

_____

I would

_____

_____

The stowaways

The two boys in the story have many adventures. Two of them are mentioned below.

✦ Read the questions and write your ideas about each event.

---

1 The two boys get into trouble at school and at home.

What did they decide to do? _____

_____

What happened? _____

_____

_____

What would you do if you were fed up with school and home?

_____

_____

_____

_____

2 The two boys find a black, rusty metal box at the beach.

What did they decide to do? _____

_____

What happened? _____

_____

_____

What would you have done? _____

_____

_____

_____

Developing literacy *Skills*

◆ The stowaways ◆

The two boys in the story have many adventures. Two of them are shown below.
◆ Read the questions and write your ideas about each event.

1 The two boys get into trouble at school and at home, so they decide to run
away to sea.
◆ Why do you think they made this choice? _____

_____

_____

The story has the following lines:

'Hardly anyone was about ... It was a very strange feeling, as if we were the only
people alive and the city belonged entirely to us. And soon the world would be
ours as well – once we'd stowed away on a ship bound for somewhere far off and
exciting!'

◆ What does this tell you about how the boys felt that morning?

_____

_____

_____

◆ Would you run away if you were really fed up? What would you do? Why?

_____

_____

_____

2 The boys found a metal box. They decide to bury it and go back for it later.
◆ Do you think this was a good or a bad decision? Explain why.

_____

_____

◆ Why do you think the parents were so upset about the box?

_____

_____

◆ What would you have done if you had found the box?

_____

_____

Overall aims

◆ To identify and discuss words and phrases that provide atmosphere, build tension and describe attitudes/emotions in stories.
◆ To write a descriptive piece of writing.

 ## *Featured book*

The Iron Man
by Ted Hughes

Story synopsis: A gigantic Iron Man arrives on Earth and begins to eat anything made of metal. Hogarth, a young boy, decides to dig a pit to capture him and with the help of the farmers, the Iron Man is caught and covered with earth, but not for long because he soon reappears. The people decide to make use of the Iron Man and they get him to eat up all the world's scrap metal. One day an enormous space dragon lands in Australia and the Iron Man helps the people to get rid of it.

 ## ◆ LESSON ONE ◆

 ## *Intended learning*

◆ To discuss and compare words and phrases used to conjure up images and atmosphere.

 ## *Starting point*

◆ Read the first chapter of the book to the children. Do they think the story is written in an exciting way? Ask them to predict what will happen.

 ## *Activity*

◆ Explain that some writers are able to make stories very exciting by the words and sentences they use. Write up some examples from the book, such as:

'The wind sang through his iron fingers.'

'All the separate pieces tumbled, scattered, crashing, bumping, clanging, down...'

'...the stars went on wheeling through the sky...'

◆ Tell the children what you like about these phrases and ask for their opinions – do the words help us to build up a picture in our minds? Do the words sometimes sound like their meaning?

◆ Working in pairs with a copy of the book, ask them to read the first chapter and note other words or phrases that they think help to describe the scene, provide atmosphere or express feelings.

 ## *Plenary session*

Bring the class together again to share their ideas. Discuss terms such as adjectives and similes and find examples of these in the chapter. Talk about how the text is arranged – sometimes very short sentences are used and at other times very long sentences with lots of commas. Discuss what these techniques might be trying to create. Which is their favourite part? Why?

Scribe a paragraph describing the Iron Man using words and phrases suggested by the children. Keep editing it until everyone is satisfied that the best words and phrases have been used. Make a large picture of the Iron Man and add the paragraph to it as a display.

Finish reading the story over the following weeks, stopping occasionally to discuss descriptive words and phrases to establish how atmosphere and feelings can be created. Copy out large versions of texts for the children to annotate – looking for adjectives, for example. Encourage them to write out descriptive phrases from their own reading to make a class display or resource bank of good phrases to use in their own writing.

◆ Intended learning

◆ To write a descriptive piece of writing linked to the use of adjectives.

◆ Starting point

Remind the children about the work carried out on Chapter 1 of *The Iron Man*. Revise their knowledge and understanding of adjectives, either by providing them with a short passage from another chapter of the book or by writing a passage on the board. Ask them to work in pairs to find the adjectives. Discuss their findings as a whole class and compare responses. Then explain that it is now their turn to write a descriptive passage using adjectives to describe a mysterious scene.

 Using the differentiated activity sheets

Provide the children with the appropriate sheet and explain the task to them. Remind them to use the most descriptive words and phrases they can think of. Encourage them to use dictionaries and thesauruses to help them find the most suitable words.

Activity sheet 1

This is aimed at those children who need a lot of support with vocabulary and sentence formation.

Activity sheet 2

This is aimed at those children who can write more independently but who need support to structure their work.

Activity sheet 3

This is aimed at more able writers who can use dictionaries with confidence and need little teacher support.

 Plenary session

After the children have completed the task, bring the whole class together again. Ask some from each group to read out their descriptions. Discuss the words and phrases used:

◆ Do they appropriately describe the scene and mystery person?

◆ Do the words used help the reader to imagine what the scene is like?

◆ Compare some of the words used. What is the difference in meaning between them? For example, big, huge and enormous.

◆ Why do some words fit but not others?

◆ What other adjectives could be used to describe the scene?

Finish by asking each child to write out their best descriptive sentence on a piece of card. Photocopy or redraw the scene from the activity sheet and add the sentences to it to make a mobile.

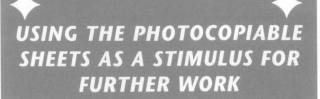

◆ ◆ USING THE PHOTOCOPIABLE SHEETS AS A STIMULUS FOR FURTHER WORK

- ✦ Use the adjectives from the sheets to begin a resource bank of describing words – make categories, such as colour, shape, size and feelings. Encourage the children to refer to the resource bank when writing.

- ✦ Use thesauruses to find other words to use instead of particular adjectives. Discuss which words would be appropriate to describe the scene and which would not.

- ✦ Use the sheets for planning a story – either by individuals or as a group effort.

- ✦ Ask the children to draw their own scene or mysterious character and write a detailed description of it – make them into a class book.

- ✦ Use the adjectives to investigate comparatives using the endings –er, –est and –ish. Discuss how this can change the meaning.

◆ ◆ OTHER IDEAS FOR USING MYSTERY STORIES

- ✦ Use descriptive extracts to discuss how the words used enable us to predict what might happen next – compare these with the use of dramatic music in films.

- ✦ Write first person accounts of the events by putting self into the story – how would you react, what would you do?

- ✦ Write a book review which discusses the credibility of the story – could this really happen?

- ✦ Write sequels using the same characters and settings.

- ✦ Read the beginning of a story and ask the children to write the ending.

- ✦ Make or find some music to go with the story – scary, suspenseful, happy and so on.

- ✦ Make mystery boxes – cover boxes and lids with paper, write words and phrases or a review of the chosen story on the paper and put the book inside the box. Display them in library or reading corner.

Developing literacy Skills

✦ A mysterious scene ✦

✦Look at this picture.

✦Put a circle round the words below that you think describe the scene and what is in it. Use a dictionary or thesaurus to add words of your own.

dark		unknown		bright
puzzling	old	strange	huge	big
scary	night	weird		happy

✦Choose words from the box to complete these sentences.

1 The _____ moon is shining down on the park.

2 A _____ man is sitting on a bench.

3 A _____ person is hiding behind a tree.

4 The person is picking up a _____ key.

5 There is a _____ suitcase near the _____ tree.

✦ On the back of this sheet, write some more sentences about this scene.
  Try to use good describing words.

✦ A mysterious scene ✦

✦ Look at this picture. Complete the writing below, using good describing words.

1 The park is dark and nearly empty. It looks _____

_____

2 An old man, sitting on a wooden bench, watches the twinkling stars in
  the black sky. The moon _____

_____

3 From behind a tree, a strange, wrinkly hand appears. It grabs _____

_____

4 Near the tree is a shiny suitcase. It _____

_____

✦ Now write some sentences about the person hiding behind the tree. Who is it?
  What does he or she look like? What is the key for? Use a dictionary or thesaurus
  to help you to collect the best words to use.

_____

_____

_____

_____

Continue on the back of this sheet.

✦ A mysterious scene ✦

✦Look at this scene. Write a detailed description of it. Try to use words that create atmosphere. You may use some of the words in the box below. Use a dictionary and thesaurus to find other words and add them to the box.

_____

_____

_____

_____

_____

_____

_____

_____

_____

_____

mysterious	frightening	weird	gnarled
decrepit	menacing		luminous
enormous		twinkling	dangerous

Using Stories
KS2: Y3–4/P4–5

Developing
Literacy
Skills

Photocopiable

39

Stories with historical settings

 Overall aims

✦ To explore settings to find clues about historical events.
✦ To use information books to cross-check these clues.
✦ To identify sequences of events in stories.

 Featured book

The War and Freddy
by Dennis Hamley

Story synopsis: This book is set during the Second World War. It recalls the events of the war through the eyes of Freddy, who is only three when war breaks out. It mentions school life, how the children formed gangs to pretend to be soldiers, fighter plane dog-fights and prisoners of war. The book only mentions the seriousness of war towards the end of the story when Freddy is confronted by news about the death of people in camps and this creates a more sombre outlook on the events. The story ends on a more hopeful note, however, with Freddy looking forward to his new life ahead.

◆ LESSON ONE ◆

 Intended learning

✦ To explore settings to find clues about historical events.
✦ To use information books to cross-check these clues.

Questions to ask

Read the first chapter and ask these questions.

Q Why do you think the trains were a mixture of different colours and types?
Q What kind of lorry would it have been if it had a red cross painted on it?
Q Why do you think Freddy was frightened by the soldiers with their sad eyes?

Q What tells you that Freddy didn't really understand what a war was?
Q Why did Freddy and his parents sleep downstairs?
Q What did Freddy think of the fighter planes that flew over his house?
Q Why do you think Freddy's mother reacted like she did when she caught Freddy outside looking at the planes fighting?
Q How do you think Freddy felt when his father went away?

 Activities

✦ Working in groups, ask the children to read through the first chapter and write down any words they do not understand. Bring the class together again to discuss the meanings of these words. Display words that are peculiar to the war era, such as 'air raid warnings', 'bombers', 'Jerries', 'Nasties', 'Messerschmitt', 'Spitfire', 'gas masks', 'army forage cap', 'Hitler' and 'call-up'.

✦ Provide some reference books and assign each group one of the following topics: air raids, fighter planes, Hitler, soldiers and gas masks.

✦ Ask each group to write down three things they know already about their topic, then three new things they have found out from reading.

Plenary session

Bring the class together and ask children from each group to read out what they knew already and then what they found out. Did finding out more information help them understand the chapter better? Is the story true to life – do the reference books back up what the author has written? How do they think their own lives at the age of three would differ from Freddy's? Discuss any problems they had using the reference books – how did they solve these problems?

It is important to finish reading the story before Lesson 2.

Developing *Literacy* Skills

◆ LESSON TWO ◆

◆ Intended learning

✦ To identify sequences of events in the story.

◆ Starting point

It is important that the whole story of *The War and Freddy* has been read before you begin this lesson.

Talk to the children about the story – was it what they expected? Do they think the author provided a good idea of what it must have been like to be a child during the war? Explain that the story chapters are dated and that the story follows Freddy's life from the beginning of the war in 1939 to the end in 1945. Do all stories go in chronological order? Can the children think of some stories where it begins in the present and then goes back to talk about the past?

◆ Using the differentiated activity sheets

Explain that you are going to challenge them to see how good their memories of the story are! Provide them with the appropriate activity sheet and explain the task to them. These activities could be suitable for paired work to enable discussion of the story sequence.

Activity sheet 1

This is aimed at those children who need support with reading and would find pictorial clues of benefit.

Activity sheet 2

This is aimed at more independent readers.

Activity sheet 3

This is aimed at the more able child who has good recall and can sequence events with confidence.

◆ Plenary session

After the children have completed the tasks, bring the whole class together as a group. Discuss their results.

✦ How difficult was it to remember the sequence of events?

✦ What helped them to recall what happened?

✦ Was it useful to work with a partner?

Discuss the story ending.

✦ How did they feel about the ending?

✦ Were they glad it ended on a happy note?

✦ If there was a sequel to the story what might this be about?

Develop the comparisons of fiction and non-fiction books as suggested in Lesson 1 further by asking questions that compare the two. For example, why did people have gas masks? Which type of book answers this more fully – fiction or non-fiction?

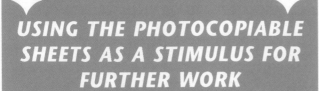

Stories with historical settings

◆ USING THE PHOTOCOPIABLE SHEETS AS A STIMULUS FOR FURTHER WORK ◆

◆ Match the dates of the story chapters to events during World War II to make a two-sided timeline – one showing what happened to Freddy and the other showing the war events.

◆ Glue the sections on to paper in the correct sequence then ask the children to write a paragraph underneath saying what they thought of the story.

◆ Make cartoon strips for each chapter showing what happened to Freddy.

◆ Make a picture book of the story by cutting up the sections in Activity sheet 2 and asking the children to draw pictures to go with each section.

◆ OTHER IDEAS FOR USING STORIES WITH HISTORICAL SETTINGS ◆

◆ Discuss what might be fact and fiction in stories – use reference books to confirm.

◆ Make puppets or dress up and act out parts of stories using the text as a reference for clothing styles, type of setting and so on.

◆ Use stories to introduce a history topic.

◆ Ask the children to write accounts linked to historical events – how would I have reacted/felt?

◆ Let the children use a story to write an historical diary, pretending to be one of the characters.

◆ Ask them to write newspaper reports of events in stories.

◆ Draw pictures of named/described objects/ artefacts from the story and use reference books to write facts about the object. Write advertisements to sell the object.

◆ Hold an 'auction' of objects made by the children of things from the story – how valuable would they be today?

◆ Discuss what might have happened if?... If the war didn't end? If electricity hadn't been invented and so on.

◆ Act out characters from stories for others to guess who it is.

Name _____

◆ The War and Freddy ◆

◆ Cut out the pictures below. Put them in the right order to show what happened in the story. Glue them on to another piece of paper.

Freddy gets a Meccano set for Christmas.

Freddy watched the soldiers get off the trains.

Freddy watched a street party.

Freddy goes to school.

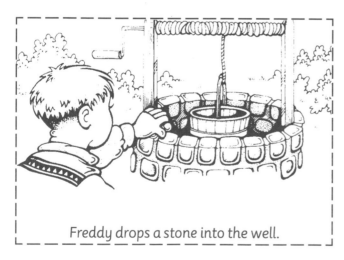

Freddy drops a stone into the well.

Freddy makes friends with a prisoner of war.

◆ Now, on another sheet draw a picture and write about something else that happened in the story.

Name _____

◆ The war and Freddy ◆

✦ Cut out the paragraphs below. Put them in the right order to show what happened in the story.

Freddy went to stay with Granny and Grandad Crake. The house was in the country and it had a well in the garden. Freddy decided to see how deep the water was by throwing in lots of stones.

The children in Freddy's street formed a gang called the South Road Army. One day Freddy found a bomb. The police and air raid wardens arrived to discover it was only an old lamp. Freddy felt very embarrassed.

Freddy stayed with his friend, Michael. They played war games but Freddy always had to be the enemy, so he tried to beat Michael at every game.

Freddy watched lots of trains bring tired men home from the war. He didn't understand what it meant because he was only three. But then his father went off to war and he began to understand.

The war ended and Freddy's father returned home. Everyone celebrated and Freddy felt he could now look forward to a happy future.

One day, Freddy went to school. He found it very difficult to learn to read and his teacher got cross with him. He soon learned, however, by reading the newspaper to try and find out about his dad.

Freddy badly wanted a Meccano set for Christmas. He was really pleased that he actually got one but he found it very difficult to use and this made him unhappy.

Freddy made friends with Marco, a prisoner of war. Marco tried to cheer up Freddy, who was worried about his father being a prisoner of war in Italy.

◆ The war and Freddy ◆

◆ Below are the chapter headings for this story. Write down two things that happened in each chapter. Then, in the boxes, write the chapters' numbers as they appeared in the book.

☐ Freddy and the prisoners of war

_____

_____

☐ Freddy and the end of it

_____

_____

☐ Freddy and the unexploded bomb

_____

_____

☐ Freddy and three sorts of water

_____

_____

☐ Freddy and the Meccano set

_____

_____

☐ Freddy and the spy

_____

_____

☐ Freddy and the start of it

_____

_____

☐ Freddy and the war games

_____

_____

☐ Freddy and the reading problem

_____

_____

Stories that raise issues

 Overall aims

✦ To identify and discuss issues raised in stories and link them to their own feelings and experiences.
✦ To respond to these issues in writing.

 Featured books

Brother Eagle, Sister Sky
paintings by Susan Jeffers
Where the Forest Meets the Sea
by Jeannie Baker
Giant by Juliet and Charles Snape
The Chicken Gave it to Me
by Anne Fine

Books synopses: The first book presents a speech given by a Red Indian leader, Chief Seattle, to the US government about the purchase and misuse of Indian land. The second is set in the rainforests of Australia and is concerned with the problem of tourist developments in areas of beauty. The third tells how people pollute and misuse the natural environment. The last story is from a battery farm chicken's point of view. Aliens come to earth and release the chickens and pen up humans instead with the intention of eating them. The story does not suggest that humans should not eat meat, but that farmed animals should have a good quality of life.

 Intended learning

✦ To discuss the issues raised in these books and relate them to their own feelings and experiences.

 Questions to ask

✦ Read the first three books to the class. (The language in *Brother Eagle, Sister Sky* is difficult so you may need to provide the children with a summary of it.) Ask the following questions to find out their ideas about the issues raised in the stories:

Q The three stories have a common idea/theme – what do you consider that to be?
Q Is there a message in the stories for the reader?
Q Why do you think the stories may have been written?
Q Is it important for children to be made aware of looking after our environment? Why?
Q Is it important to protect our forests and areas of natural beauty? Can you give reasons why?
Q Do the illustrations in the books help to give the message? How?
Q Has the arrival of people from other countries affected the lives of people such as Aborigines and Red Indians? How?
Q Does this affect our environment?

 Activities

✦ Divide the children into pairs or small groups and ask them to make two lists:
1 Five things that people do to harm the environment (mention two from the stories);
2 Five ways we can help to look after our environment today.

 Plenary session

Bring the whole class together again to share the ideas. Ask some children to read out their lists – do others agree? Make collaborative lists of all the ideas as a class record.

Discuss how harmful acts can affect our own lives. What are the children's feelings about how the environment is treated? How does this affect their futures? Do people have a choice in how they behave towards the environment? Have they had any personal experiences of seeing the effects of actions on the environment – either good or bad?

What could be done with the two lists? Could they write to people about particular local issues or make posters to tell others how to look after the school and local area?

◆ LESSON TWO ◆

◆ Intended learning

◆ To identify and discuss the issue raised in the story *The Chicken Gave it to Me*.
◆ To write a letter to a character in response to the issue.

◆ Starting point

Read the story before the lesson. Remind the children about the discussions earlier concerning caring for our environment. Ask them to tell you if they think this story also has a message about our environment.

◆ Key questions

Q What do you think the story is trying to tell us?
Q Is it important to look after animals in our care? Why?
Q Would the chicken be happy to live on a free range farm?
Q What parts of the story help you to decide your answer?
Q If humans were farmed, what ideal conditions would we need?
Q Why do you think battery-hen farms were set up in the first place?
Q Does the farmer have a real choice about farming methods used today?

◆ Using the differentiated activity sheets

Explain to the children that they will now have an opportunity to respond to the issues raised in the story by writing a letter. Discuss how to set out and write letters correctly. Share ideas about the type of letter to be written – it is not a chatty letter to a friend but has a specfic purpose. Stress the importance of using evidence to back up argument.

Activity sheet 1

This is aimed at those children who need support with vocabulary and how to set out a letter.

Activity sheet 2

This is aimed at more independent writers.

Activity sheet 3

This is aimed at more able writers who are capable of using information books independently. Stress to these children the need to make the letter business-like yet helpful, as well as ensuring that each question is answered.

◆ Plenary session

After the children have completed their letters, bring the whole class together to share their work. Explain the task that each group had to complete. Ask some children from each group to share their letters.
◆ Discuss each letter in turn.
◆ Did the letter do what it was meant to do?
◆ Did the writer include enough information?
◆ Do you agree with what the writer has said?
◆ What problems did you have writing the letter?
◆ How could the letter be improved?
◆ How can letters help us to express our opinions?

Stories that raise issues

USING THE PHOTOCOPIABLE SHEETS AS A STIMULUS FOR FURTHER WORK

✦ Ask the children to respond to each other's letters, pretending to be the farmer, the chicken and Gemma and Andrew. What might their responses be? Share the replies to see how similar/different they are.

✦ Use the word list on Activity sheet 1 to start a brain-storm of words to describe battery-hen farming and free-range farming. Use the words to make posters about each type of farming method. Try to present the good and bad aspects of each type.

✦ Use the letters as a starting point for descriptive pieces of writing. Ask the children to write down adjectives to describe how the chicken might feel on battery-hen and free-range farms. Use the adjectives to write sentences or a paragraph about how the chicken might feel.

✦ Role-play the chicken, the farmer and the children. What might they say if they met in a court of law. How would they present their case about battery-hen farming? Their letters could be used as evidence!

- • How To Cope With Bullies •
- • Tell your friend
- • Tell your teacher
- • Tell your family
- • Ask for help
- • Don't be a bully

OTHER IDEAS FOR USING STORIES THAT RAISE ISSUES

✦ Use the books to locate evidence for and against an issue. Discuss these views.

✦ Read stories from different countries/cultures – how do the issues raised compare with the children's own country/culture?

✦ Change the endings of stories by resolving the issue in a different way.

✦ Discuss why the children think these kinds of stories are written. Is it good to raise issues in stories? How does it help us? Could it cause problems sometimes?

✦ On some cards, write some issues such as bullying, bereavement, and making difficult decisions. Ask the children to draw a card from a hat. They could write their own story about it or use it as a stimulus for class or group discussion. Ask them if they know of a story about this issue. How did the story help them to understand the problem more? Have they experienced this problem? How did they overcome it? What/who helped them?

✦ Use the issues from stories to write 'Help' posters for others to read. For example, 'How to cope with bullies', 'What to do if you fight with your best friend' and 'How to help someone who is sick'.

✦ Build up a list of stories about particular issues. Encourage the children to add to the list each time they read a book. Display the list in the reading corner and library so that the children can select particular books when an issue concerns them.

Developing literacy Skills

✦ Letter to the farmer ✦

Write a letter to the battery-hen farmer at Harrowing Farm.
Here are some ideas to help you:
✦ Say what you think about this type of farming.
✦ Tell the farmer how it affects the chickens.
✦ Suggest some better ways of keeping chickens.

Dear Farmer
I am writing to you about the farming of your chickens.
I think

Write your own address or school address here. Write the date underneath.

Complete the letter in your own words.

Sign your name here.

Here are some words you may want to use. Add some more of your own.

feathers	stretch	cramped
scratch	dreadful	cruel
free-range	pecking	build
clean	people	wonderful

◆ Letter to the chicken ◆

Write a letter to the chicken to thank her for writing the story about Harrowing Farm. What do you think you should say? Here are some ideas:

◆ Tell her what you have learned about battery-hen farming.
◆ Tell her what you think about her visiting the aliens.
◆ Tell her how you think her story might help people.

Dear Chicken

Write your own address or school address here. Write the date underneath.

Complete the letter in your own words.

Yours sincerely

Sign your name here

Developing literacy skills

Photocopiable

◆ Letter to Gemma and Andrew ◆

After reading the story about the chickens at Harrowing farm, Gemma and Andrew wrote to Green Care, an Environmental Group, to find out how they could help. This is the letter they wrote.

◆ Imagine you are the manager of Green Care. Write back to Gemma and Andrew, answering their questions.

> 10 Farmview Court
> Hillside Valley
> Tumbletown
>
> 22 January 1998
>
> The Manager
> Green Care
> 29 Smith Street
> Localtown
>
> Dear Sir/Madam
> We are concerned about the treatment of farm animals and would like to help. Please could you answer the following questions:
> 1. How do we know when we buy farm products from the shops that the animals have been well looked after?
> 2. How can we let other people know about the good and bad things about battery farms?
> 3. How can we find out what people in our community think about this?
> 4. How can we find out if people would buy free-range foods or not?
>
> Yours faithfully

Write your letter here.

Overall aims

✦ To introduce the children to a range of different stories as part of a series.
✦ To discuss how the books are similar in writing style, characters, book layout.
✦ To write another book in the series.

 ## Featured books

The Happy Families series
by Allan Ahlberg

Story synopsis: This series of easy-to-read books contains stories about different families who have different hobbies or occupations. Many words and phrases are repeated throughout the stories to help the reader become familiar with them. There is always a problem to solve in the story and each story uses lots of illustrations throughout. Many of the stories challenge gender stereotyping.

 ## ✦ LESSON ONE ✦

 ## Intended learning

✦ To introduce the children to the *Happy Families* series.
✦ To discuss how the books are similar.

 ## Starting point

Hold up several titles from the series. Ask the children if they have read any of these books before. Do they know who wrote them? Are they familiar with other titles by this author? Explain that the *Happy Families* books are from what is called a series because the books are all about families and they are written in a very similar way. Do the children know any other series of books written by other authors?

 ## Activities

Tell the children that they are going to work in a small group to find out how the books in the series are similar. Provide three or four children with two or more titles each. Ensure that each group has an able reader to help read the stories. Ask them to discuss the following:

✦ Are the illustrations similar? In what way? Are they all colourful? Do they use speech bubbles? Are some of the pictures framed? Are there pictures on every page? Do some pictures take up a whole page?
✦ Is the story about a family? What kind of family? What jobs do the adults have? Are there always children in the family?
✦ Does the family have a problem to solve? What is the problem? How do they solve it? Is there a happy ending?
✦ Does the author use mainly long or short sentences? Does he use speech in the writing? How is the writing set out on the pages? Is it similar in each book? Does each book have the same number of pages?
✦ How are the cover pages the same? Are the back pages similar? How?

 ## Plenary session

Bring the whole class together to share what they found out. Act as scribe to write a whole class list of things that are similar about each book. Does everyone agree on the list? Has anything important been left out? Why do they think books in a series need to be so similar? If they like the format and type of story in a series, does it make them want to read more of them? Make a display of the books together with the agreed list of things that make the stories similar.

◆ LESSON TWO ◆

◆ Intended learning

◆ To write another book in the *Happy Families* series as a collaborative group effort.

◆ Starting Point

Summarise what the children have found out about the *Happy Families* series; how the books look, what kinds of characters are in the stories, how a problem is solved and so on. Tell them that they will now work in groups to write a *Happy Families* story of their own.

◆ Points to consider

Ask them to consider the following things as they work in their groups:

◆ How will they decide on the story? Will they share their ideas and then choose the best one or will some people work on the beginning, the middle or the ending?
◆ Who will write it? Will there be a group scribe, will each person write the story in full or will each person write part of the story?

◆ Will the group make one book or each person make their own version of the same story?
◆ Who will do the illustrations? Will each person do some each?

◆ Using the differentiated activity sheets

Activity sheet 1

This is aimed at those children who need support with story ideas and would benefit from having illustrations as a guide.

Activity sheet 2

This is aimed at those children who are able to use text clues but need help in structuring a story.

Activity sheet 3

This is aimed at children who are more able writers and who need less structure to plan their story.

◆ Plenary session

After each group has written their stories, bring the whole class together and discuss the following:

◆ What problems did they have in writing the story?
◆ Do they feel that they worked together well as a group? If they did have problems working together how did they solve them?
◆ Ask some children to read out their stories. Do the others think they fit in with the series well? Can the others help to improve it in any way?
◆ Finally, allow more class time to make the stories into individual or group books. Copy the front and back cover designs and book size of the *Happy Family* series.

USING THE PHOTOCOPIABLE SHEETS AS A STIMULUS FOR FURTHER WORK

✦ Use the activity sheet as a model for the children to make up their own *Happy Families* characters for further book writing.

✦ Write other adventures in the lives of Mrs Snip, Miss Sparks and Master Air.

✦ Write a diary of the event, pretending to be one of the characters, for example Mrs Snip's account of her hairdressing disaster.

✦ Use reference books to find out about the 'real' day-to-day roles of an electrician, hairdresser and balloonist.

✦ Use the pictures from Activity sheet 1 to act out a play about the story.

✦ Make the pictures from Activity sheet 1 into a cartoon strip.

✦ Ask each child to draw a different picture for the middle part of the story about Master Air. Ask them to write or tell the different story and how it ends.

OTHER IDEAS FOR USING STORIES IN SERIES

✦ Act out a character from a series. Can the others guess who it is and what book it is from?

✦ Make up a play about the stories which includes characters from different books in the series.

✦ Draw characters from different books. Can the children match them to the correct story?

✦ Hot seating. Ask the children to become a character from a book. Can the others ask questions to try and work out who it is?

✦ Change the ending of a familiar story.

✦ Ask the children to say which book they like best in the series and explain why.

✦ Write letters from a character in one book to a character in another book.

✦ Write stories with lots of characters from the series all in one story.

✦ Read very short extracts from each book – can the children guess the series title?

✦ Draw the head of one character joined to the middle of another and to the bottom of a third character. Display this and ask the children to work out the three characters involved.

✦ Mrs Snip, the hairdresser ✦

✦ Cut out the pictures below. Put them in the right order to tell the story. Glue them onto a piece of paper and write a sentence underneath each one to say what is happening.

✦ Miss Sparks, the electrician's daughter ✦

✦ Complete this story about Miss Sparks by filling in the gaps.

This is Miss Sparks.

She lives with her parents who are

electricians. Mr and Mrs Sparks have

always been _____.

Their mothers and _____ were

electricians too. Miss Sparks wanted to be

an electrician as well.

One day she decided to fix the

_____. But the problem was that she couldn't

_____. So she tried to

_____, but that didn't work. So the next day

she went to _____ and bought a _____. She used

it to try and fix the _____. Suddenly, _____

_____ !

Mr and Mrs Sparks ran into the room. They were not very _____ but

they decided to help their daughter. Together, they _____

_____.

Soon it was all fixed and Miss Sparks was very _____. But then

something terrible happened. She accidently tripped over the _____.

In the end, Miss Sparks decided never to go near a _____ ever again!

Name _____

✦ Master Air, the balloonist's son ✦

✦ Use this page to write your story about Master Air. Make the story into a book with pictures.

The beginning	Introduce Master Air and his family. Write about the things they like to do and how they live. Describe the balloon.

The middle	This is what happens to Master Air. How did he get there? What other things happened before he landed on the whale?

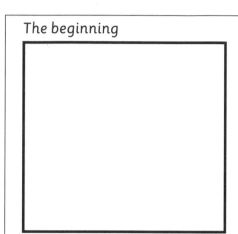

The end	How did Master Air escape from the whale? What happened next?

Using Stories
KS2: Y3–4/P4–5

Developing
literacy
Skills

Photocopiable

57

Book reviews

Overall aims

- To make children aware of the common features of books – title, author information, publisher details, illustrations, contents pages, book presentation.
- To provide opportunities for children to express their own opinions about books and author/ illustration styles.

Featured books

A collection of different books by Allan Ahlberg, such as **Peepo!, The Cinderella Show, The Giant Baby, The Jolly Postman, Please, Mrs Butler**

LESSON ONE

Intended learning

- To discuss book presentation and structure.
- To compare books by the same author.
- To give opinions about format and author style.

Starting points

- Provide each child with a story book (not from the Ahlberg collection). Ask them to locate the following information – author, title, publisher and illustrator. Show them where the publisher details are and talk about the reasons for the different dates shown for publication. For example, the first one is usually in hardback, sometimes books are updated, if the book is very popular it will be re-printed and so on.
- Compare cover presentation – is the title in the largest print or the author's name? What attracts them to pick up a book – a well-designed cover, a well-known author or a striking title?
- Look at the back cover. Discuss the information found there – price, ISBN number, bar code, author information, story summary, comments about the book. Do the children refer to the back cover before reading/choosing a book?

- Compare how the books present several pages before the story starts – is there a chapter or contents page? Has the author written a comment or a dedication? Are other titles written by the same author listed somewhere?
- Next, show the children the collection of books by Allan Ahlberg. Compare the different types of book presentation – cut-outs, envelopes, cartoon style, novel format, lots of illustrations, very little illustration and so on. Ask the children to give you their opinions about each type – Do they like it? What age group would it attract most? Why? Why do they think one author has written in so many different styles and formats? Would a particular format put them off reading a book? What can we learn about this author from this collection of books?

Activity

Divide the children into five groups. Provide each group with a collection of different books by different authors in the following categories:

- books of different sizes
- books with different types of illustrations
- books in different formats – pop-ups, lift-the-flaps
- books with very different cover designs
- books with different text layouts

Ask each group to appoint a scribe and a spokesperson to present their findings to the rest of the class. Then ask them to discuss the following:

- which design/type they like best/least and why
- which one is the most unusual/least common
- how important do they think book size and illustration are to attract readers.

Plenary session

Bring the class together again and ask the spokesperson for each group to report back. Discuss any issues that are raised and talk about what it is that attracts them to particular books.

Developing Literacy Skills

◆ LESSON TWO ◆

◆ Intended learning

◆ To write a book review.

◆ Starting point

Explain that you would like the children to choose a book to write a review. Remind them where to find book conventions such as author, title and publisher. Provide them with a role model for writing a review by telling them about two books you have read – one you really enjoyed and one you didn't like so much. Tell them what you think of the book cover, illustrations, presentation and story. Explain that it is not necessary to enjoy every book you read and that sometimes you may not enjoy one from your favourite author – this is how we develop our reading tastes and learn what we like and do not like. What is important, though, is for the children to learn how to identify why they haven't enjoyed a particular book. Book reviews are one way of developing this because they encourage the sharing of ideas about positive and negative responses to books.

◆ Using the differentiated activity sheets

Provide the children with the appropriate activity and ask them to select a book to review.

Activity sheet 1

This is aimed at those children who are less able at reading and writing and may need teacher support.

Activity sheet 2

This is aimed at those children who are more confident writers.

Activity sheet 3

This is aimed at more able children who are able to express their opinions in writing more fully.

◆ Plenary session

Share some of the children's responses with the whole class. Do others agree with their opinions? Discuss how it is possible for one person to really like a book and another person to hate it. Ask the children to tell you their current favourite author and explain why they like him/her. Make a class graph of the results to put in the reading corner along with the completed book review sheets.

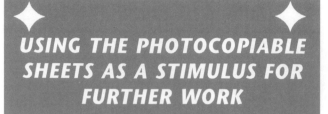

Book reviews

USING THE PHOTOCOPIABLE SHEETS AS A STIMULUS FOR FURTHER WORK

✦ Photocopy some of the completed sheets and cut off the information about title and author. Can others guess the book from reading the review?

✦ Find out more information about the authors using reference sources. Make a book or wall display about the author with information, a list of titles written and a book review.

✦ Ask five children a week to write a review of a book in the class or school library – display them as an information source for others.

✦ Send the reviews to the author for his/her comments.

OTHER IDEAS FOR USING BOOK REVIEWS

✦ Write to authors or publishers to obtain first-hand information and answers to questions.

✦ Carry out a school survey to find out the most popular authors, favourite book presentation style and so on. Graph the results and make the findings public.

✦ Have a school book week to raise the focus of books.

✦ Have an author of the week/month and relate reading activities to this author.

✦ Write reviews on book characters – how credible are they?

✦ Rearrange books in the reading corner into authors to enable children to locate titles more easily.

✦ Make a scrap book of newspaper articles, book blurbs and so on about favourite authors.

✦ Invite an author/illustrator into school to find out how they go about their work, where their ideas come from and so on.

✦ Carry out a book conference with each child once a term to discuss in detail their opinions and reading habits.

✦ Read extracts from books not read by the class to introduce them to new authors.

Developing
literacy
Skills

Activity 1   **Name** _____

✦ My book review ✦

TITLE _____ AUTHOR _____

✦ Circle your answers about this book.

1 Do you like the story?   Yes   No

2 Do you like the pictures?   Yes   No

3 Is the story –   boring   funny   sad   scary   exciting   happy

4 Do you like the cover?   Yes   No

5 Is the story set in –   the past   the present   the future

6 How would you rate the book? Excellent   Very good   Good   OK   Poor

✦ In the box below, draw or write about something that happened in the story.

✦ Write what you like about this book.

_____

_____

✦ Write what you don't like about this book.

_____

_____

✦ Would you read other books by this author?   Yes   No

✦ Would you tell others to read this book?   Yes   No

◆ My book review ◆

TITLE _____ AUTHOR _____

Draw a picture here of a character from this book.

Who is the main character?

_____

What is the story about?

_____
_____
_____

What do you like about the story?

_____
_____

What don't you like about the story?

_____
_____

Would you tell others to read it?

Yes ☐   No ☐

How do you rate the story? Tick the boxes.

Excellent	☐	Exciting	☐
Very good	☐	Boring	☐
Good	☐	Funny	☐
OK	☐	Sad	☐
Poor	☐	Scary	☐

Do you like the cover?

Yes ☐   No ☐

Say why _____
_____
_____

Does the book have pictures?

Yes ☐   No ☐

Are they:

colour	☐	black & white	☐
large	☐	small	☐
good	☐	poor	☐

Do they:

help tell the story ☐

not help tell the story ☐

If you like the pictures, say why.

_____
_____

Developing Literacy Skills

Activity 3

Name _____

✦ My book review ✦

TITLE _____

AUTHOR _____

ILLUSTRATOR _____

PUBLISHER _____

DATE OF FIRST PUBLICATION_____   ISBN _____

Where does the story take place? _____

Who are the main characters? _____

_____

What is the story about? _____

_____

_____

What kind of story is it?   Adventure ☐   Mystery ☐   Everyday ☐

Fairy tale ☐   Myth/legend ☐   Science fiction ☐   Horror ☐

Historical ☐   Humorous ☐   Factual ☐   Fiction ☐

Give your opinion about the story. Would you recommend it? Why/why not?

_____

_____

Comment on the cover. Is it a good design? _____

_____

Have you read other books by this author? If so, is this one as good as the others or better/worse? Why? _____

_____

Does the book have illustrations? ☐ Say what you like or dislike about them.

_____

How do you rate the story?

Excellent ☐   Very good ☐   Good ☐   OK ☐   Poor ☐

Acknowledgements

The following is a list of all the children's storybooks that have been referred to in this book as the basis for literacy work.

- ◆ *The Secret Garden* by Frances Hodgson Burnett (Puffin, 1981)

- ◆ *Danny the Champion of the World* by Roald Dahl (Puffin 1986)

- ◆ *I'll take you to Mrs Cole* by Nigel Gray and Michael Foreman ((Macmillan Children's Books, 1987)

- ◆ *Chocolate Fever* by Robert Kimmel Smith (Pan Books, 1989)

- ◆ *The King's Equal* by Katherine Paterson (Harper Collins, 1992)

- ◆ *The Orchard Book of Greek Myths* retold by Geraldine McCaughrean (Orchard, 1992)

- ◆ *The Stowaways* by Roger McGough (Viking Kestrel, 1986)

- ◆ *The Iron Man* by Ted Hughes (Faber & Faber, 1986)

- ◆ *The War and Freddy* by Dennis Hamley (Scholastic Publications, 1994)

- ◆ *Brother Eagle, Sister Sky* by Susan Jeffers (Picture Puffins, 1993)

- ◆ *Where the Forest Meets the Sea* by Jeannie Baker (Julia Macrae, 1987)

- ◆ *The Chicken Gave it to Me* by Anne Fine (Methuen, 1992, reprinted by permission of Reed Consumer Books)

- ◆ *Giant* by Juliet and Charles Snape (Walker Books, 1990)

- ◆ *Happy Families* series by Allan Ahlberg (Puffin Books)